10,000 Tears

10,000 Tears

*The Second Coming
in First Thessalonians*

By Dr. Lee Roberson

Sword of the Lord Publishers
Murfreesboro, Tennessee 37130

Printed and bound in the United States of America

Table of Contents

The Gracious Heart

"But I would not have you to be ignorant, brethren, concerning them which are asleep, that ye sorrow not, even as others which have no hope."—I Thess. 4:13.

As I begin another series of messages on the second coming of Christ, I must express my thanks to the illuminating Holy Spirit and to the friends who directed my thinking on this truth some thirty-five years ago.

In the early part of my ministry, I had read my New Testament through a number of times. I had read the Greek New Testament from the first word of Matthew to the last word of Revelation and signed a pledge to this effect in the class of Dr. A. T. Robertson in the Southern Baptist Theological Seminary. Yet, I knew nothing of the truth of the second coming.

The small note that I had inscribed on the top margin of Revelation 20 had little significance. Some teacher had said, "Don't be pre- or post-—be *for* the second coming—that's enough."

Then in my second pastorate, I began to read and reread my Bible. My attention was drawn to the very familiar portion of the verse in John 14:3, "I will come again." I decided to preach on this but knew nothing about the meaning of the verse and of the great fact of the return of Jesus.

I again began reading every verse in the New Testament and I placed a mark by the side of each verse that referred to the second coming (I put the two letters S. C.). I secured some books on the great fundamental doctrines and began to read them.

Then there came the day when I preached my first sermon on the second coming. I saw at once the mighty working power of the Holy Spirit in my life and in the lives of others. I saw how the Lord could use this truth to glorify Himself and to point people to the Lamb of God.

Now let us turn back to the six verses that I have chosen to use for the seven messages on the second coming.

Paul was concerned for his people. It is evident that the Thessalonians had been disturbed by some teaching on this subject. Word had come to the apostle regarding the matter; and, hence, he wrote to them under the guidance of the Holy Spirit. Graciously, he pointed them to the Son of God and to the promised return.

He assured their hearts regarding their deceased loved ones, and he also stirred the living to look for Christ.

Paul said, "The promise is plain. Jesus said He would return, and He will."

"For the Lord himself shall descend from heaven with a shout, with the voice of the archangel, and with the trump of God: and the dead in Christ shall rise first."—I Thess. 4:16.

The proof is positive. The Word of God has spoken. Our Saviour has declared the fact that He will return and will receive us unto Himself.

Again, the preparation is personal. We are to live in readiness for the return of our Saviour. The event is certain, but the time is uncertain. Just when Jesus will appear is one of God's secrets. No man can mark off a certain day and say, "He must appear on this time." But the question is, "Are you ready for His coming?" Are you living in the light of His return? John tells us, "And every man that hath this hope in him purifieth himself even as he is pure."

The term "the second coming" is not used in the Bible. But it is implied by the writer of the Hebrews in this phrase: ". . .unto them that look for him shall he appear the second time. . ." (Heb. 9:28).

Quickly, let me state that our Saviour's coming is one event but in two stages. He will first come in the air to receive us unto Himself. This we call the "rapture"—the snatching away. Second, He comes with the saints down to this earth, here to reign upon the earth as King of kings. The first stage is His private manifestation. The second stage is His public manifestation.

We should believe His coming. Here is the promise of it: "For if we believe that Jesus died and rose again, even so them also which sleep in Jesus will God bring with him" (I Thess. 4:14).

We should pray for His coming. John did so, and we should do so. "Even so, come, Lord Jesus."

We should love His coming. Paul wrote to Timothy:

"Henceforth, there is laid up for me a crown of righteousness, which the Lord, the righteous judge, shall give me at that day: and not to me only, but unto all them also that love his appearing."

We should watch for His coming. Paul said this in I Thessalonians 5:6, "Therefore let us not sleep, as do others; but let us watch and be sober."

We must live for His coming. "For our conversation is in heaven; from whence also we look for the Saviour, the Lord Jesus Christ" (Phil. 3:20). Our obligation is to live so as to be unashamed to stand before Him.

Here is a truth for everyone: for young people, for the middle aged, for the elderly. Here is a truth for the poor, the middle class, and the rich. The gracious heart of the Apostle Paul was reaching out to the people of his day and to us, also, that we might have joy as we anticipate the coming of our Lord.

Now think of this truth.

I. THIS IS THE TRUTH
THAT ENERGIZES

No one can debate the energy and dedication of the early Christians. They moved out on the command of Christ. They worked; and as they worked, they looked for His return. Jesus promised the power of the Holy Spirit as they went. On the same day that our Saviour ascended into glory, the two heavenly beings repeated unto them the truth of the return of Jesus Christ.

"And while they looked stedfastly toward heaven as he went up, behold, two men stood by them in white apparel;

"Which also said, Ye men of Galilee, why stand ye gazing up into heaven? this same Jesus, which is taken up from you into heaven, shall so come in like manner as ye have seen him go into heaven."—Acts 1:10,11.

Here we find the energy of the Apostle Peter. He knew the Saviour. He heard His words. He heard the promise of His return. Therefore, we find nothing but boldness in the ministry of this one from the day of Pentecost on. He stood before the enemy without fear. He preached without favor.

This truth energized the ministry of the Apostle Paul. From the day that Christ appeared to him on the road to Damascus, to the day that he died for his Saviour, Paul was energized by the truth of the return of the Saviour. In every writing of the apostle mention is found of the second coming.

Think of the energy of John. This man was stirred by the truth of the Saviour's return. With clarity, he preached it through his writings. Notice these words:

"And now, little children, abide in him; that, when he shall appear, we may have confidence, and not be ashamed before him at him coming."—I John 2:28.

"Beloved, now are we the sons of God, and it doth not yet appear what we shall be: but we know that, when he shall appear, we shall be like him; for we shall see him as he is."—I John 3:2.

The book of Revelation has one great message, the coming of Christ.

"Behold, he cometh with clouds; and every eye shall see him, and they also which pierced him: and all kindreds of the earth shall wail because of him. Even so, Amen."—Rev. 1:7.

From the first to the last, this is the book that tells us of the coming of our Christ. It tells us that He is coming for us, to receive us unto Himself. It tells us that He is coming to this earth for the battle of Armageddon, for the judgment of living nations, and for the establishment of His millennial reign on earth.

In this truth of the second coming, we find the energy of James, in the practical book that bears his name. He said, "Be patient therefore, brethren, unto the coming of the Lord." And again he said to the people, "Be ye also patient; stablish your hearts: for the coming of the Lord draweth nigh."

This is the truth that energizes! An illustration of this would come from the ministry of Dr. Mark Matthews of the First Presbyterian Church of Seattle, Washington. For more than thirty-five years Dr. Matthews pastored the church. He was a dignified, scholarly man. Every year for thirty-five years he gave a series of sermons on the truth of the second coming. Through much of this time he repeated the same messages. But throughout all of the time, large crowds packed the big auditorium to hear the eloquent Matthews. A caretaker in the building told me there were occasions when people were admitted to the second coming series only on ticket.

The caretaker also informed me that scores of people were saved Sunday after Sunday as Matthews preached on the second coming of Jesus Christ.

II. THIS IS THE TRUTH THAT ILLUMINATES

Here is a truth that helps men understand the Word of God. It is my conviction that no one can come to a full understanding of the Word of God unless he reads it with his mind open to this truth—the second coming of Christ.

The great Bible teachers, evangelists, pastors, and lay-Christians have all held to the return of Jesus Christ. I am thinking of that noble Christian, Dr. I. M. Haldeman, pastor of the First Baptist Church of New York City. This man became world famous through his preaching of the truth and through the publication of many volumes of sermons.

This truth illuminates the Word! The second coming is mentioned 318 times in the 260 chapters of the New Testament. It occupies one in every twenty-five verses from Matthew through Revelation. In the Old Testament there are repeated promises of the return of Jesus. We are told that He is coming to die as Saviour. Most of the promises refer to His coming to reign as King.

For many people this doctrine of the second coming might seem unnecessary and impractical, but not so. This truth will illuminate your mind and heart and will give you understanding of the great truths of the Word of God.

Dr. R. A. Torrey said:

> There have been four marked epochs in my Christian experience: First, when I came to know the Lord Jesus as my personal Saviour and my Lord. Second, when I discovered that the Bible was indeed the inerrant Word of God, that its statements were absolutely reliable in every respect, and that everything any man needed to know was contained in this one Book. Third, when I learned that the baptism of the Holy Spirit was for the present day and claimed it for myself; and fourth, when I came to see the truth concerning the second coming of Christ. The latter truth transformed my whole idea of life. It broke the power of the world and its ambition over me and filled my life with the most radiant optimism, even under the most discouraging circumstances.

III. THIS IS THE TRUTH THAT COMFORTS

The portions of the Word of God that we read at funerals deal with the second coming of Christ. I have listened to modernistic preachers read portions containing this truth. They read them without understanding and without any effort to comfort others.

In John 14:1-6, a beautiful portion that we read so many times, we find the promise of His coming, "I will come again, and receive you unto myself; that where I am, there ye may be also."

In I Corinthians 15, we read of the resurrection. But the great emphasis of the chapter is upon verses 51 to 58. Here is the part that tells us that He is coming "in the twinkling of an eye . . . and the dead shall be raised incorruptible, and we shall be changed."

In II Corinthians 5:1-10, we find plain and evident mention of His return. The last verse tells us that "we must all appear before the judgment seat of Christ; that every one may receive the things done in his body, according to that he hath done, whether it be good or bad."

In I Thessalonians 4:13-18, we are plainly told these words are given to comfort us: "Wherefore comfort one another with these words."

In Revelation 21 and 22, we are pointed to the coming of the Lamb of God. We read about Heaven, about the beauty of the place being prepared for us, and the passage closes with the words, "Even so, come, Lord Jesus. The grace of our Lord Jesus be with you all. Amen."

Here is the one truth that God commands us to use for comfort. Shall we allow modernism to take this from us? Modernism flatly denies the premillennial second coming. Shall we take the infidelic way of a Bishop Pike or a Bishop Robinson? These men are notorious for their denial of the Word of God and of the truth of the return of Jesus Christ.

No, we must follow the Word, for here is the truth that comforts. It has ever been the comfort of the child of God. "It was his comfort when he was made to fight the wild beasts in the arenas of Rome; or when he worshiped Christ, the Lamb of God, in the catacombs. It was his comfort when tortured in the dungeons and prisons of the Inquisition." It is his comfort in the "concentration camps and extermination camps of the Hitlers and Stalins or in the underground assemblies behind the Iron Curtain today."

I believe with all of my heart that wherever and whenever Christians have to face suffering and death, they are comforted by the assurance of His coming and the hope that they will receive from His hands a new body, a new life, a glorious future.

IV. THIS IS A TRUTH THAT CENTERS ON CHRIST

He is the One who is coming again.

Great will be the benefits to us, but He is the One who is coming to receive us unto Himself.

He is the One we long to see.

He is the One who will wipe away our tears.

He is the One who will equalize the inequalities of life.

He is the One who shall reign upon the earth as King of kings and Lord of lords.

Now, as the second coming centers on Him, the second coming turns us unto our Lord and gives us peace and joy.

A little church magazine coming to my desk a few days ago had these words about the coming of Christ.

First, it is a signified event. We do not know when He is coming, but we are to be watching for the coming of our Saviour.

Second, it is a silent event. He will come as "a thief in the night."

Third, it is a sudden event. He will come "in the twinkling of an eye," when men least expect Him.

Fourth, it is a shocking event. Many will be shocked when the Saviour comes. Our Lord Jesus said, "Then shall two be in the field; the one shall be taken, and the other left" (Matt. 24:40).

Fifth, it is a separating event. The saved will be caught up. The unsaved will be left. It will separate the real from the hypocritical. It will separate good from evil. It will separate the saved from the unsaved.

I bid you to center your thinking now upon our Lord Jesus. He is the One you need in this moment of time. He is the one for you to know, for He may come at any time! He is the Saviour you need, for death might strike at any moment.

Some years ago I assisted Dr. Melvin C. Eidison in a revival meeting in the First Baptist Church, Bessemer, Alabama. Dr. Eidison would often recount a story regarding a boy named Wesley Vincent.

Wesley Vincent was taken in by a more experienced criminal. He joined a man by the name of Richard Darrafou. They began to rob the business houses of Birmingham, Alabama.

They were in the act of robbing the cash box in a store when a Birmingham policeman by the name of Harris walked in. Instantly, one of the men killed Harris. Darrafou was actually the one who did the crime, but he cheated the law by committing suicide. Young Vincent took another course entirely. It was his first crime. He saw not only the folly but the enormity of his iniquity and confessed it all.

His mother, being a Baptist, sent for Dr. Eidison, and Eidison led the boy to Christ. And the lad said, "I have found peace." He said, "I can never forgive myself for the sorrow and shame I have brought to my darling mother, but God has in His mercy forgiven me."

When his mother came to comfort him just before he was led to the death cell, he begged her not to cry. He admitted his guilt. He deplored the awful gravity of it. He said, "My punishment is perfectly just." But he affirmed, "I have sought and found both pardon and peace."

He walked unassisted to the death chair. He subjected himself to the straps that bound him to the death-dealing electrodes. And with a smile, he bade his mother and Dr. Eidison goodbye.

The daily press report gave his last words addressed to the executioner. Here they were:

> I am looking at you now, but my eyes are actually on Christ my substitute, my Saviour. I am being punished for what I did, but I know God has forgiven me. I am ready.

Dr. Eidison prayed. The reporter said silence fell over the death chamber. A few minutes later physicians stepped forward. Putting the stethoscope against Vincent's bare breast they said, "He is dead."

Who saved the lad? The Lord Jesus Christ. Let us center all of our thinking upon Him. He is our Saviour, and He is our coming King.

"Watch therefore: for ye know not what hour your Lord doth come."—Matt. 24:42.

Ten Thousand Tears

"*. . .that ye sorrow not, even as others which have no hope.*"—I Thess. 4:13b.

This is a world of tears—tears of pain, tears of disappointment, tears of frustration, tears of broken hopes, tears of sorrow.

To the tearful, weeping world Paul says:

"*But I would not have you to be ignorant, brethren, concerning them which are asleep, that ye sorrow not, even as others which have no hope.*"—I Thess. 4:13.

Paul is saying that death is common. We will shed tears when loved ones go from us. But in your sorrow, keep your eyes upon the fact of a coming Lord Jesus. For when He comes, death will be no more; and we shall be in His presence.

"Furthermore," Paul says, "the lost world has no hope. Do not sorrow as those which have no hope."

"Ten Thousand Tears." I am using an expression to get you to see the heartache of the world and to help you to see our greatest hope—the coming of Christ.

Today there are tears because of uncertain conditions in the Middle East, in Palestine, in Russia, and in many other parts of the world.

Tears are everywhere! Here is a language that is understood by all. Tears and weeping mean sorrow in any language in every part of the world.

The great God who made all things loves us. Though He holds the world in His hands, He is conscious of the tears of the weakest saint.

If we are to be Christlike, we too must shed tears over a lost world. Jesus did. Paul did.

Sin should bring tears, whether over our sins or another's. Jeremiah wept because of the sins of Israel. Let us not become calloused in heart. Don't take sin as an ordinary matter. Sin is against God. God hates sin.

Yes, tears are everywhere. Someone said:

> The measure of one's soul is to be found in the things that make one weep. Esau wept for the loss of his heritage. Israel wept in the desert for the leeks and garlic of Egypt. Delilah wept to make Samson tell her his secret. Hezekiah wept because he was about to die. David wept for Absalom. The scarlet woman wept at the feet of Jesus for her sins, and Peter wept because he had denied his Lord. Jesus wept over lost and doomed Jerusalem. Tears may be the most selfish or the most saintly things in the world. Jesus asked Mary beside the tomb: "Why weepest thou?"

We try to build a world of laughter, and we fail miserably. Our homes are in trouble. Our nation is in trouble. Lost mankind is in trouble.

We try to drink ourselves out of trouble, and get into more of it.

We try to work ourselves out of difficulties, and get into more difficulties. We think that money is a way out. More money is being spent to damn the world than to save it. Millions are spent, not every year, not every day, but every hour in the ghastly business of sin. Our nation is billions of dollars in debt and going deeper all the time. Crime is increasing daily, and more money is spent on crime than on anything else.

I saw this introduction to a write-up in a missionary magazine. It said, "Americans now spend 200 million dollars annually for foreign missions. That sounds like a lot, but did you know that we spend more than that for chewing gum?"

We try to sing our way out of trouble, and the more we sing, the deeper we get. "Music has charms"—but music fails without a saving relationship with God.

We try to ignore death, and we hope to relieve ourselves of some trouble. A member of our church went to work on last Friday. A few minutes after eight he was found dead by another member of our church.

Death is the unwelcome visitor. There comes a knock at the door. "Who is there?"

The answer: "I am—Death."

"But I didn't send for you."

"I know you didn't, but I have come, and you must go with me."

"But I am not ready to go."

"You have had all your life to get ready. Come, you have only three minutes."

"But I can't go. Don't come so close to me. Don't breathe your cold breath in my face."

"One minute. . .ten seconds. . .five. . .four. . .three . . .two. . .one," and the undertaker is on his way.

There is only one blessed hope for all of us—the second coming of Christ. What joy, what satisfaction, what a soul-thrilling thought to know that one day He is coming, and we shall be in His presence.

Now with this introduction, I think you can understand how Paul could write, ". . .sorrow not, even as others which have no hope."

I. SORROW NOT—THERE IS COMING A RETURN OF CHRIST

Jesus said, "I will come again." Here is the sweetest thought in the entire Bible. Heaven is near. Jesus is near. The "home over there" is near. Christ is coming again!

Try to imagine that day when Jesus stood with His disciples outside Jerusalem and gave to them the Great Commission. Then the cloud received Him out of their sight. They stood there looking stedfastly toward Heaven, watching the Saviour as He went up. And "behold, two men stood by them in white apparel." These men said, "Ye men of Galilee, why stand ye gazing up into heaven? this same Jesus, which is taken up from you into heaven, shall so come in like manner as ye have seen him go into heaven."

Jesus said He would come again. The two heavenly beings said He would come, but the fact of His second coming is repeated in every part of the New Testament. More than three hundred times in the New Testament is the coming of Jesus Christ given unto us. Not only in the New Testament, but in the entire Bible we are promised the return of our Saviour.

Now if plain language means anything, then it simply means that Christ is coming again. Paul believed the statement of our Lord Jesus and he said, "The Lord himself shall descend from heaven with a shout, with the voice of the archangel, and with the trump of God. . . ."

Some people would try to get you to believe that death is the second coming. Not so, for the Bible says "the Lord himself." When Christ comes, the dead in Christ shall be raised. When death comes for the Christian, no dead person arises.

Some try to say that regeneration is the second coming of Christ. But Jesus said, "I will come again, and receive you unto myself." It is a wonderful thing when sinners are regenerated, when they are made new people in Christ Jesus. But the salvation of a sinner is not the second coming.

Some have held to the fact that the coming of the Holy Spirit was the second coming of Jesus Christ. But not so! On the day the Holy Spirit came, there was no resurrection of the dead, no changing of the believers. Jesus Christ is coming again, and we must be ready for this glorious coming of our Saviour.

Now, the time of His coming is indefinite, but the coming is imminent. This means that He may come at any moment, and we must be ready and watching for the coming of our Saviour.

II. SORROW NOT—THERE IS COMING A RESURRECTION

"For the Lord himself shall descend from heaven with a shout, with the voice of the archangel, and with the trump of God: and the dead in Christ shall rise first."—I Thess. 4:16.

Death is not the end—it is just the beginning for the child of God.

Death brings the Christian into the presence of God. Paul gives us a word regarding this in II Corinthians 5:6-8.

"Therefore we are always confident, knowing that, whilst we are at home in the body, we are absent from the Lord:
"(For we walk by faith, not by sight:)
"We are confident, I say, and willing rather to be absent from the body, and to be present with the Lord."

But dying and going to be with the Lord is not all; there is coming a resurrection. That which is sown in corruption shall be raised in incorruption. That which is sown in dishonor shall be raised in glory. That which is sown in weakness shall be raised in power.

There is coming a resurrection and we shall receive resurrection bodies like the body of the Lord Jesus Christ.

"Beloved, now are we the sons of God, and it doth not yet appear what we shall be: but we know that, when he shall appear, we shall be like him; for we shall see him as he is."—I John 3:2.

We shall have bodies like that of our Lord Jesus Christ. They will not be subject to sickness and death. These bodies will not know the limitations and deficiencies of this life. Every limitation, every defect is to be left in the grave.

What a marvelous prospect is this for every one of us! At the resurrection, the blind will have sight. The lame will walk; the weak will be made strong. These vile bodies shall be changed like unto our Saviour's glorious body, perfect in every part.

One day the Saviour will come. When He comes, He will bring with Him the souls of all who died with their faith in Him. At His coming, the body, sown in corruption, will be raised in incorruption. The resurrection body and the eternal soul are brought together for eternity.

III. SORROW NOT—THERE IS COMING
A RAPTURE

"Then we which are alive and remain shall be caught up together with them in the clouds, to meet the Lord in the air: and so shall we ever be with the Lord."—I Thess. 4:17.

The dead are raised, and the living are caught up—". . .and so shall we ever be with the Lord."

When He comes, these bodies will be changed; and our bodies will be made like His. Let us read this in Philippians 3:20,21.

"For our conversation is in heaven; from whence also we look for the Saviour, the Lord Jesus Christ:

"Who shall change our vile body, that it may be fashioned like unto his glorious body, according to the working whereby he is able even to subdue all things unto himself."

We feel the limitations of our present bodies, and we are waiting for our adoption, "to wit, the redemption of our body."

When will this body be redeemed? When our Saviour comes. In that moment, we shall have a body like unto His own glorious body.

The days of weariness and weakness will be forever at an end. The body will be able to accomplish all that the spirit purposes.

The body will be free of limitations. It will be a heavenly body.

Dr. W. B. Riley used to say that this time when our bodies are made like the body of Christ that we will take a journey—first into Heaven, into the heavens where we shall celebrate the marriage supper of the Lamb.

Our second journey will be back to this earth. We are coming with our Saviour, as He comes for the battle of Armageddon and the judgment of living nations and for the establishment of the millennial reign. We shall reign with our Saviour for a thousand years upon this earth before we go into the new heavens and the new earth, there to be with Christ forever.

The rapture—the snatching away—is a time when we shall be caught up to be with our Saviour.

Paul said, "Behold, I shew you a mystery; We shall not all sleep, but we shall all be changed" (I Cor. 15:51).

One generation of Christians will be living when Jesus Christ comes. They will be given bodies like unto the body of the Saviour.

The graves will open. The living will be changed, and together we will be caught up into His presence. Do not allow this to mystify you. We live in a strange and interesting day when many mysterious things are happening. This is the day when pictures and words fly through the air. Radio and television are everywhere. This is the time of startling speeds through God's heavens. This is God's world. He made it all, and He is sending Christ to receive us unto Himself.

IV. SORROW NOT—THERE IS COMING A REUNION

". . .and so shall we ever be with the Lord."—I Thess. 4:17b.

Separation is the order of this day. There will be a great separation when Jesus comes, we are very plainly told. The Saviour said, "Then shall two be in the field; the one shall be taken, and the other left." When Jesus comes, the saved will be caught up and the unsaved will be left. The tragedy of the Great Tribulation we will deal with at a future date, but I am concerned now about this reunion. There will be a reunion with our loved ones in Christ. First, a reunion with Him, our blessed Saviour. What a blessed prospect is this!

Then we shall have a reunion with our dear ones who are on the other side waiting for us.

Can you think of loved ones on the other side? Loved ones whom you long to see? Many have gone out of this church, and I surely want to see them face to face—our many faithful deacons, ushers, Sunday school teachers, choir members, and many who were just faithful members. My friend, there is coming a reunion!

I want to see again our Dr. Charles Weigle. He was ninety-five when he left us. But when we see him, he will be like the Lord Jesus Christ. Praise God, we shall be like the Saviour ourselves! Dr. Weigle used to love to sing his song:

> I would love to tell you what I think of Jesus,
> Since I found in Him a friend so strong and true.
> I would tell you how He changed my life completely.
> He did something that no other friend could do.

He would sing also his song entitled "Oh, What Glory!" These were songs of anticipation, songs of longing; but one day we shall see him. There will be a song of eternal joy upon his lips.

How beautiful is the thought of Heaven.

In the land of fadeless day
Lies the city four-square,
It shall never pass away,
And there is "no night there."

And the gates shall never close
To the "city four-square,"
There life's crystal river flows,
And there is "no night there."

There they need no sunshine bright,
In that "city four-square,"
For the Lamb is all the light.
And there is "no night there."

God shall "wipe away all tears";
There's no death, no pain, nor fears;
And they count not time by years,
For there is "no night there."

What is the hope of this world? The hope is Jesus Christ, the Lamb of God, who takes away the sin of the world.

Christ is our hope for this present day. Atheism builds no hospitals. Agnosticism sends out no missionaries. Infidelity does not reach in the darkened corners of the world. These things come from those who believe in Jesus Christ, the Son of God.

The world of today is in a sad and deplorable state. Society has been shaken to its very foundations. Civilization is rocking. The economic systems of the world are weak. We talk about peace, but we fight wars. We talk about peace, but we send thousands of our boys into the war-torn areas of this sinful world.

What is the simple remedy of the entire situation? It is Christ Jesus, the Saviour.

God has a plan for every life.

Step number one is for you to come to Christ and be saved. "For whosoever shall call upon the name of the Lord shall be saved."

Step number two is for you to be submissive to the will of God.

Step number three is for you to be watching for His coming.

Do you know the Saviour? Are you ready for the coming of Jesus Christ? You can be made ready by one simple act. Repent of your sin and believe in Jesus Christ, the Son of God.

The Greatest Word in
the World

"For this we say unto you by the word of the Lord. . . ."—I
Thess. 4:15.

We often hear people say, "Just what can you believe in this
day?" Or, "Whom can you believe in this hour?"

Falsehoods are common. Lying is a practice in many businesses. In the *Saturday Evening Post* was an article entitled
"New Traffic in Cures for Cancer." The story tells us of hundreds
going to Tijuana, Mexico, to be cured of cancer. In this "shabby
city of illusions," cancer patients are given treatments ranging in
cost from $10 to $50. Some people have cancer. Some do not. But
the doctors of Tijuana urge the same treatment for the "same"
money.

How refreshing it is to come to the Bible, God's holy Book.
Every word is true. Every promise is reliable. This Book has been
proven true by the centuries. This Book has been vindicated by
the tests of millions.

Now Paul said, "For this we say unto you by the word of the
Lord. . . ."

Yes, Paul knew what Christ said about the second coming. He
knew that Jesus said, "Watch therefore, for ye know neither the
day nor the hour wherein the Son of man cometh" (Matt. 25:13).
He knew that Jesus said, "I will come again, and receive you
unto myself; that where I am, there ye may be also."

But that wasn't all. The Holy Spirit inspired the pen of Paul
and directed his writing of the words of this paragraph of sacred
Scripture. This was the Word of God directly given to Paul.

"For this we say unto you by the word of the Lord, that we which are alive and remain unto the coming of the Lord shall not prevent [or precede] them which are asleep.

"For the Lord himself shall descend from heaven with a shout, with the voice of the archangel, and with the trump of God: and the dead in Christ shall rise first:

"Then we which are alive and remain shall be caught up together with them in the clouds, to meet the Lord in the air: and so shall we ever be with the Lord."—I Thess. 4:15-17.

This was the Word as revealed unto Paul. The Word of God is sure and stedfast.

Perhaps we wonder sometimes why the second coming is not preached more. We might ask the same question about the preaching of salvation by grace, eternal security, the infallibility of the Scriptures, the filling of the Spirit, death to self, and many other subjects.

Men turn from the Word of God to human reasoning. They prefer in many cases the word of man to the Word of God.

At a National Council of Churches meeting in Dallas, Texas, Dr. Kelly Brubaker Culley, dean of the New York Theological Seminary, told a group of church workers that "Sunday school is on the way out—at least in the long run."

Culley said that the public schools might take over the task of teaching biblical history, literature and philosophy. If this is done, then the church could concentrate on "living religion." He urged religious educators to revise new approaches "to make it possible for people to become really involved in the life and practice of religion."

The need of the hour is to get back to the Bible! This is the need of the National Council of Churches. It is the need of all of our churches. Modern philosophy and modern teaching methods have never succeeded in saving souls and building Christian character. The Bible must be taught, believed and followed.

Now let us consider what Paul says to us in I Thessalonians 4:15:

I. THE WORD SAYS THAT HE WILL
COME AGAIN

No one can read the Word of God even lightly without being impressed with His promised return.

First, He will come, for He said so. If He does not come, then every other word given by the Saviour would be false also. But the Saviour said that He would return, and this He will do.

Second, the time of His coming is uncertain. We are not to set times. The Bible tells us, "Therefore, be ye also ready: for in such an hour as ye think not the Son of man cometh" (Matt. 24:44).

In the first century there were some who were setting times regarding the return of Jesus. This has upset many Christians all through history. People have been setting time regarding the return of the Lord. William Miller had it fixed beyond the peradventure of a doubt for the year 1843. He had his followers put on white ascension robes and wait for the moment when they would be caught up into the air. But nothing happened. They merely changed the date and said that Christ would come a year from that time, but still nothing happened.

Michael Baxter, Professor Piazzi Smyth, Mr. Dimbleby, Charles Taze Russell, Judge Rutherford, and many others have made prophecies of the return of Jesus Christ, but again nothing happened.

No man knows the hour. Let the "time-setters" beware. The time is in the Father's hands. The angels do not know. The apostles in glory do not know. Only the Father knows.

Third, the accompanying events are sure. He is coming again. The dead in Christ shall rise first, and then the living shall be changed. How blessed it is to contemplate that which is going to transpire when our Saviour appears.

His coming will bring to pass all the prophecies of a better world—a golden age. He will come to receive us unto Himself and then we will come with Him down to the earth for the reign of Christ. In this age the Saviour will reign as King of kings and Lord of lords. Crime, oppression and wickedness will be put down. Swords will be beaten into plowshares. Spears will be made into pruning hooks. The peace that man has ever longed for will come to the earth. But remember, this peace will come only with the coming of the Lord Jesus Christ.

II. THE WORD TELLS US OF WORLD CONDITIONS WHEN HE COMES

"And as it was in the days of Noe, so shall it be also in the days of the Son of man.

"They did eat, they drank, they married wives, they were given in marriage, until the day that Noe entered into the ark, and the flood came, and destroyed them all.

"Likewise also as it was in the days of Lot; they did eat, they drank, they bought, they sold, they planted, they builded;

"But the same day that Lot went out of Sodom it rained fire and brimstone from heaven, and destroyed them all.

"Even thus shall it be in the day when the Son of man is revealed."—Luke 17:26-30.

The wickedness of the days of Noah and the days of Lot will be known in the day of the coming of the Son of man.

Let us turn to II Timothy 3:1-5 and notice what we find regarding the days preceding His coming.

"This know also, that in the last days perilous times shall come.

"For men shall be lovers of their own selves, covetous, boasters, proud, blasphemers, disobedient to parents, unthankful, unholy,

"Without natural affection, trucebreakers, false accusers, incontinent, fierce, despisers of those that are good,

"Traitors, heady, highminded, lovers of pleasures more than lovers of God;

"Having a form of godliness, but denying the power thereof: from such turn away."

Now, what about world conditions when He comes?

First, the world will be in a time of awful sin. Sin is on the increase. Sin will continue to increase until the coming of our Lord. The postmillennial doctrine presented the idea of steady spiritual improvement until the coming of Christ. This is pretty much out of the way, but still there are people who will talk about improving conditions. There are still some who believe the world is getting better and better. The Bible leaves no doubt regarding the day of His coming. Study your Bible regarding the time of Noah and of Lot.

Second, the day of His coming will be a day of sleepy, sinful unconsciousness. That is the reason Paul gave the admonitions of I Thessalonians 5. Listen to his words:

"But of the times and the seasons, brethren, ye have no need that I write unto you.

"For yourselves know perfectly that the day of the Lord so cometh as a thief in the night.

"For when they shall say, Peace and safety; then sudden destruction cometh upon them, as travail upon a woman with child; and they shall not escape.

"But ye, brethren, are not in darkness, that that day should overtake you as a thief.

"Ye are all the children of light, and the children of the day: we are not of the night, nor of darkness.

"Therefore, let us not sleep, as do others; but let us watch and be sober.

"For they that sleep sleep in the night; and they that be drunken are drunken in the night.

"But let us, who are of the day, be sober, putting on the breastplate of faith and love; and for an helmet, the hope of salvation."—I Thess. 5:1-8.

Again, in the day of the coming of our Lord, there will be scoffers. Peter tells us:

"Knowing this first, that there shall come in the last days scoffers, walking after their own lusts,

"And saying, Where is the promise of his coming? for since the fathers fell asleep, all things continue as they were from the beginning of the creation."—II Pet. 3:3,4.

Another indication of this day is given to us by the Lord when He said, "Then shall two be in the field; the one shall be taken, and the other left. Two women shall be grinding at the mill; the one shall be taken, and the other left."

Third, in the coming of our Lord, there will be a falling away from the faith. There will be a turning from simple faith in the Bible.

"Let no man deceive you by any means: for that day shall not come, except there come a falling away first, and that man of sin be revealed, the son of perdition;

"Who opposeth and exalteth himself above all that is called God, or that is worshipped; so that he as God sitteth in the temple of God, shewing himself that he is God."—II Thess. 2:3,4.

In the time of the coming of our Lord there will be many who will try to exalt themselves by saying, "I am Christ."

There will be "wars and rumours of wars" throughout this entire age; and even unto the coming of our Saviour, nation will still be rising up against nation.

Of course, our political leaders cannot understand these truths which come to us from the Bible. When the President placed a wreath upon the Lincoln Memorial marking Abraham Lincoln's birthday last Monday, he said:

> Lincoln stuck it out, sad but steady. So will we. In Lincoln's spirit, we will achieve a just and a lasting peace among ourselves and among all nations.

In the *Fort Wayne Journal* there appeared an editorial a few years ago. It was entitled "The Search for Peace." It read as follows:

> The greatest task before the world in this generation is to find the way to peace on earth and good will among men.
> And there is little time to lose.
> After World Wars I and II, the world was in a mood for peace. Statesmen gave a solemn promise.
> The United Nations was founded and charged with the business of keeping men and nations from crippling or destroying themselves in armed combat.
> There was at that time as now the threat of the hydrogen bomb hanging over the head of the world.
> But the job has proved too big for the United Nations— although it has helped the cause of peace in some instances.

The spirit of peace has not descended upon the earth.

Today almost every nation is seething with trouble—including our own.

It is apparent that treaties and organizations cannot bring peace by themselves. Peace must be in the hearts of people everywhere and they must convince their leaders that peace with justice and fairness is what they want.

How long are the leaders of mankind going to continue to travel in the old ways of diplomacy which lead to war?

Why do they not listen to the voices of the great teachers of religion and philosophy who have spoken down through the ages pleading for the nations to adopt the good neighbor policy and live as friends in harmony?

Let us remember the promises which were made to the people after the two greatest wars and try with all our might to carry them into practice.

If peace can reign upon our planet then we can solve the other problems which perplex us in this latter half of the twentieth century.

An editorial of that kind is thoughtless and without any scriptural foundation. It is as foolish as "today's prayer," which I saw on the front page of a daily newspaper:

Our Heavenly Father, please receive our most humble thanks for the many blessings you have bestowed upon our nation. Guide our leaders and the leaders of all nations to the peace table where they will break bread together and enjoy brotherly love throughout the world. Amen.

I return to my first statement. The Bible tells us of world conditions before He comes. There will continue to be wars and rumors of wars. Sin will increase. Man will live in his wicked unconscious state. He will fall away from the faith. But praise God, the Saviour is coming!

III. THE WORD TELLS US THE TRUE ATTITUDE WE MUST HAVE TOWARD HIS COMING

First, the Bible says that we are to be ready for the coming of our Lord. This is pressed upon us by many portions of the Word of God. Christ is coming "in such an hour as ye think not." We know not the hour of His coming; therefore, we must be ready every day and every moment.

Second, we must be watchful. The Bible says, "Watch therefore." We are not taught in the Word of God to watch for death, but to watch for His coming. True watching welcomes Him. We are to be watching and ready. This means that we will turn from any task to meet our Saviour. We shall rejoice to see Him.

Third, we must be busy at the coming of our Lord. We must engage in the work that He has left us to do. How rich is this truth! We must work as we watch for His return.

A successful businessman, fifty years of age, took me to the airport last evening. He said, "I was at my work at 5:00 a.m. today." He went on to tell about how many hours he spent per day at his work and quite often even seven days of the week. I complimented him on his busy schedule, but I pointed out that he needed also to be busy for the Saviour.

Fourth, we must be witnessing for Christ. We must let our light shine for Him. Jesus said, "Ye shall be witnesses unto me." We must constantly tell the story of Jesus and His power to save.

The second coming of Christ does not take away from our soul winning. Rather, it adds to it! It should not diminish our zeal but should contribute to our zeal to bring people to the Saviour.

Dr. William Biederwolf, one of my favorite preachers of days gone by, had the following to say:

> What a soul-thrilling thought to know that someday and doubtless soon, the Lord of glory is coming again. The Lord by whom all things were made; the Lord who stretched out the firmament like a silver canopy in the sky; and pinned back the curtains of the night with clusters of stars; the Lord who set the pillars of the earth in their sockets, lifted up the mountains and wrapped them in robes of clouds and set the lakes like huge crystals studded with emeralds among the green pockets of the hills—this Lord, the Lord who came to earth from the glory which was His before the world was that He might redeem it from the curse that came with sin—the Lord, whose godlike wisdom filled the doctors of the temple with astonishment, whose healing touch made the lepers clean; who said, "Peace

be still" to the wild fury of the storm-swept sea; who laid His hands in blessing on the little ones—the Lord of Gethsemane's bloody sweat, of Calvary's iron spikes, of the broken tomb, and of the cloud that received Him out of their sight.

This is the Lord who is coming—coming to vindicate the sure word of Holy Scripture as spoken of His many prophets of old.

Coming to silence forever every argument concerning Himself and to show to the world that the One who hung on Calvary's cross was really the Son of the living God.

Coming to establish peace and righteousness where the unsanctified efforts of men have wrought only envy and suspicion, class hatred, and war, with every form of wickedness and oppression in general.

Coming with a shout and with the voice of the archangel to wake the dead and transform His living saints into the likeness of His own glorious body and gather them to Himself in the air.

Are you ready for His coming? Do you know that Christ is your Saviour? Are you living daily in such a way that you would be happy to be caught into His presence?

The Lord God offers us so much: be sure that you don't refuse the gift that God offers you.

Many of you have read the story this week of Clint Wescott. Mr. Wescott is fifty-one years of age and has been "on the bum" for fifteen years.

He refused $19,219. He said, "Hand me a dollar. I'll take it. Buy a little drink, a little smoke; but I don't want the $19,219. I just don't want the money."

Wescott sleeps in the weeds in a vacant downtown lot in Los Angeles. He had forty-four cents in his pocket when the money was offered to him. It was money that belonged to him from the sale of property that he had back in New York State.

Many of you would say, "What a foolish man!" Yes, he is foolish, for with the money that is his, he can pull himself out of the dirt, grime and filth of his life and can live respectably.

My friend, how foolish also is the man who refuses the great gift of salvation! Man grovels in the dirt and filth of this world seeking for peace and happiness. At the same time, he turns his back upon the Son of God who offers salvation, life, peace and joy forevermore.

The invitation is for you. Will you receive Jesus Christ as your Saviour? Will you receive the gift of everlasting life? "For the wages of sin is death: but the gift of God is eternal life through Jesus Christ our Lord" (Rom. 6:23).

The World's Greatest Shock

"For the Lord himself shall descend from heaven with a shout, with the voice of the archangel, and with the trump of God: and the dead in Christ shall rise first:

"Then we which are alive and remain shall be caught up together with them in the clouds, to meet the Lord in the air: and so shall we ever be with the Lord."—I Thess. 4:16,17.

Tucked away in I Corinthians 13:10 is a little portion of a verse that I want to bring to your attention in the opening of this sermon.

"But when that which is perfect is come. . . ." Here is a prophetic statement. We are going toward perfection.

We now live in the midst of an imperfect world, but we are assured of coming perfection. In an atmosphere of world discontent, we are told there is coming a world of perfect peace.

The present world is marred by sin. The world grows increasingly sinful and farther from God each day. This is the fulfillment of the prophecy given to us in this Book. There is no promise in the Bible of perfection and righteousness for this age. We are told of gradually increasing sinful conditions up to the time of His revelation.

We are informed that wars and rumors of wars will continue. Kingdom shall rise against kingdom.

We are admonished to make our choice—whether to follow a sinful, doomed world, or to follow Christ who will one day be King of kings and Lord of lords.

The sinfulness of this age is before us now. The Bible reveals that which is going to take place. One day the Great Tribulation will come upon the world. The work of the world dictator is outlined for us in the Bible. At the end of the tribulation, there will be the battle of Armageddon. After that, then the judgment of living nations will take place. Following this, we come to the reign of Christ for a thousand years, a reign of righteousness upon this earth. Then will come a shadow for a time, a brief uprising as pictured in Revelation 20:7-10, and the Great White Throne Judgment as described in Revelation 20:11-15.

Revelation 21 and 22 bring us to the new heavens and the new earth. Here is God's picture given to us:

"And I heard a great voice out of heaven saying, Behold, the tabernacle of God is with men, and he will dwell with them, and they shall be his people, and God himself shall be with them, and be their God.

"And God shall wipe away all tears from their eyes; and there shall be no more death, neither sorrow, nor crying, neither shall there be any more pain: for the former things are passed away.

"And he that sat upon the throne said, Behold, I make all things new. And he said unto me, Write: for these words are true and faithful."—Rev. 21:3,4,5.

But now I come in this message to discuss with you "the world's greatest shock."

The world is becoming less and less susceptible to shock.

War is common.

Death is common. Newspapers tell us of scores killed in the everyday pursuit of life.

Dissension is common, dissension that spreads from the capitals of nations down to the humblest hamlet.

Accidents are common. People are shocked but little by the variety of accidents which are found in every part of our nation.

Every day we hear and see the shocking: but tonight I want you to think of "the world's greatest shock." I am dealing specifically with the two verses which I have read as the text for this sermon, verses that tell us of the time when "the dead in Christ shall rise first" and "then we which are alive and remain shall be caught up together with them in the clouds, to meet the Lord in the air: and so shall we ever be with the Lord."

I. THE MAGNIFICENCE OF THE OCCASION

I hold before me God's infallible Word! I point out to you that there is coming the day when Jesus will "descend from heaven with a shout, with the voice of the archangel, and with the trump of God: and the dead in Christ shall rise first"! What an amazing and wonderful day this will be! What a magnificent time when the graves will be opened and the dead in Christ shall be raised!

But not only so; here is another magnificent thing. The living will be changed and caught up in the air to meet the Lord. Let me give you three words to tie together this occasion.

First, resurrection. The Lord will come. The dead in Christ shall rise first. What is this? The first resurrection. We read the following in Revelation 20:6,

"Blessed and holy is he that hath part in the first resurrection: on such the second death hath no power, but they shall be priests of God and of Christ, and shall reign with him a thousand years."

The Bible speaks of two resurrections. The first is when Jesus comes for His own; the second is when the unbelieving dead are brought before the Great White Throne Judgment. We are dealing now with the magnificence of the occasion when the dead in Christ shall be raised. What an awesome picture is this! What a stirring, dramatic occasion is ahead of us! Graves will be opened, and those who died with their faith in Christ will come forth.

Second, think of the word "translation." "Then we which are alive and remain shall be caught up together with them in the clouds. . . ." Paul is demonstrating to us in this portion how to speak of the second coming of Jesus Christ. This is the way that we should ever speak of it—"Then we which are alive and remain. . . ." We are to be looking for His coming every day. We are to expect a shout from Heaven.

We are going to be changed. We are going to be made like our Lord. This is what Paul said in I Corinthians 15:51-53:

"Behold, I shew you a mystery; We shall not all sleep, but we shall all be changed,

"In a moment, in the twinkling of an eye, at the last trump: for

the trumpet shall sound, and the dead shall be raised incorrupti-
ble, and we shall be changed.
"For this corruptible must put on incorruption, and this mor-
tal must put on immortality."

Don't allow your limited, worldly, finite mind to pull away
from these challenging, magnificent statements. This is given us
by the Lord Himself. He spoke through the Apostle Paul and has
given to us words of comfort.

Third, reunion. "And so shall we ever be with the Lord." This
is reunion. We are going to see our Lord, and we are going to be
with our loved ones. I repeat, "And so shall we ever be with the
Lord."

This is the end of the battle as we know it here. This is the end
of the ceaseless struggle that man has in this present world. We
are coming into the presence of our Christ, and we shall be with
Him and with those who know Him throughout eternity.

This simple portion of the Word brings to light another
beautiful thought, and that is that we shall know each other in
Heaven. Not only in this portion of Scripture but in many places
the thought is given unto us. For example, David had no doubt
about knowing his child in Heaven. He said, "But now he is
dead, wherefore should I fast? can I bring him back again? I shall
go to him, but he shall not return to me" (II Sam. 12:23).

The Apostle Paul also indicates that we shall know each other
in the presence of our Lord. For he said, "For what is our hope, or
joy, or crown of rejoicing? Are not even ye in the presence of our
Lord Jesus Christ at his coming? For ye are our glory and our
joy" (I Thess. 2:19,20).

We have an interesting little portion of the Word of God given
to us in Philippians 4. Paul spoke of three people whose names
were "in the book of life." He named them—Euodias, and Syn-
tyche, and Clement. These three had little differences in opin-
ions about certain things, but Paul very tenderly sent a word to
them and told them to be of the same mind. And he frankly said,
"Your names are in the book of life." Paul is indicating that
these three will be in Heaven with our Lord and that they will

know each other in Heaven. Since this is true, they should be "of the same mind."

There is another evidence to the fact that we will know each other in Heaven. That is given to us in the picture of Christ on the Mount of Transfiguration. You recall that Peter recognized Moses and Elijah who came down and talked with our Lord.

The conversation between our Saviour and the men from Heaven was scarcely started when Peter said, "It is good for us to be here: and let us make three tabernacles; one for thee, and one for Moses, and one for Elias. . ." (Luke 9:33).

I remind you that Moses died some 1,400 years before this time. I remind you also that Elijah had been translated about 800 years before; and yet when these two came down to talk with our Lord, the Apostle Peter knew them.

I give all of this just to emphasize "the magnificence of the occasion." Christ is coming. The dead will be raised. The living will be changed and translated and we shall be together with the Lord in the air.

II. THE SHOCK OF THE OCCASION

The dead are going to be raised, and the living are going to be changed. There will be a definite shock to this occasion. In a world that is just about shock-proof, there will still be something shocking about this. This, I believe, will be the "world's greatest shock."

Perhaps I should not say it, but it seems to me that some Christians may be shocked. Why? So many are not looking for the coming of our Lord. Even those who have heard the message of the second coming have still failed to make themselves ready, and to be watchful, in the event that He comes at any moment.

Again, some are saved and have heard nothing of the second coming of the Lord Jesus. Perhaps their salvation has been so recent that they have not had the opportunity to hear of His coming. But when He comes, they will be caught up. The dead will be raised, the living changed, and "caught up together with them in the clouds, to meet the Lord in the air."

But the greatest shock of all will be to the unsaved world. Here
is what our Saviour said:

*"I tell you, in that night there shall be two men in one bed; the
one shall be taken, and the other shall be left.*

*"Two women shall be grinding together; the one shall be
taken, and the other left.*

*"Two men shall be in the field; the one shall be taken, and the
other left."*—Luke 17:34-36.

There is no way to measure the shocking elements of this occasion. All of the electronic devices of the world would fail in
measuring the thing that is going to happen.

The first reaction that may come from those who are left would
be this: "What has happened?" They will discover that many are
gone from their midst. Homes are divided. Businesses are dis-
rupted. A friend is gone. A loved one is suddenly no more. What a
shocking time, when men will be crying, "What has happened?
What is the meaning of all this?"

And I believe there will also be a second reaction—the
troubled will be saying, "Why did this happen?" Some may even
cry, "Why didn't someone tell us about this? Why didn't
someone inform us about the coming of the Lord Jesus? Why
didn't someone tell us about this great separation?"

A third reaction—some will cry, "What can we do?" Oh, the
Holy Spirit has been caught away when believers were snatched
from this earth. I believe the Bible will be left among men and
that some will turn to the Word of God; and that by a definite
personal working of the Holy Spirit upon their hearts (as the
Holy Spirit worked in the Old Testament days) they will come to
a knowledge of Jesus Christ and salvation. It has ever been my
belief that some will be saved in the tribulation days.

*"And one of the elders answered, saying unto me, What are
these which are arrayed in white robes? and whence came they?*

*"And I said unto him, Sir, thou knowest. And he said to me,
These are they which came out of great tribulation, and have
washed their robes, and made them white in the blood of the
Lamb."*—Rev. 7:13,14.

The world's greatest shock will be when Christ shall come for His own. It will be shocking to schools, to homes, to businesses, to churches. It will be a shock to Congress, to the United Nations, to the governments of the world. It will be a shock in the bars, honkytonks, dance halls, houses of ill fame. There may be a small awakening in some of these places, but what a shock will come when God takes out His own!

I am reminded of the simple story given by a man who said he had been discussing the second coming with his wife. He had read the Bible and studied very carefully the matter of the coming of our Lord and of the great separation. They had talked about the Scripture that says, "One shall be taken and the other left."

After discussing the matter for some time, they put the children to bed and then they retired. Later in the night, one of the children began to cry. The wife arose and went into the next room to the side of the child.

After the wife had gone from the room, the husband awoke. When he found his wife gone from his side, suddenly there flashed into his mind the Scripture they had been discussing, "One shall be taken, and the other shall be left."

This is the time to think through this matter! I know of wives who are fine, devoted Christians, and husbands who are rebellious, scoffing sinners.

There is coming a time of separation.

III. THE MEANING OF THE OCCASION

Every prophecy in the Word of God will be fulfilled. Christ is coming again to receive us unto Himself. In His coming, we will see the beginning of the fulfillment of all promises.

We will be brought into His presence. We will come to the realization of our fondest dreams.

What does the second coming of Jesus Christ mean for us? Simply this: we shall reign with Him.

"Do ye not know that the saints shall judge the world? and if the world shall be judged by you, are ye unworthy to judge the smallest matters?

"Know ye not that we shall judge angels? how much more things that pertain to this life?"—I Cor. 6:2,3.

What is the meaning of the occasion? What should we do as we think of this coming event? We must first live for Christ and be prepared to stand before Him. We must, second, do our best to win others to the Saviour. We must be ready for the rapture when our Saviour comes for us. Jesus said, "Be ye also ready: for in such an hour as ye think not the Son of man cometh." We must keep these words in mind daily.

Every morning when we arise we should say to ourselves, "Perhaps today the Lord is coming." Every night we should repeat, "Would I be ready for my Lord's return if He should come before I awake in the morning?"

In preparation for His coming, we must live lives that are separated from the world. Notice this warning given by the Lord Jesus in Luke 21:34-36:

"And take heed to yourselves, lest at any time your hearts be overcharged with surfeiting, and drunkenness, and cares of this life, and so that day come upon you unawares.

"For as a snare shall it come on all them that dwell on the face of the whole earth.

"Watch ye therefore, and pray always, that ye may be accounted worthy to escape all these things that shall come to pass, and to stand before the Son of man."

In preparation for His coming, we must daily be filled with the Holy Spirit. "And be not drunk with wine, wherein is excess; but be filled with the Spirit" (Eph. 5:18).

Daily we should be working for Him. "Therefore, my beloved brethren, be ye stedfast, unmoveable, always abounding in the work of the Lord, forasmuch as ye know that your labour is not in vain in the Lord" (I Cor. 15:58).

And finally, we must be looking for Him.

"Watch ye therefore: for ye know not when the master of the house cometh, at even, or at midnight, or at the cockcrowing, or in the morning:

"Lest coming suddenly he find you sleeping.

"And what I say unto you I say unto all, Watch."—Mark 13:35-37.

My friend, are you ready for the coming of the Saviour? Do you know that you are saved by His grace?

He is coming again. I think that we will be surprised at some who will "go up" when He comes and some who will not be caught up. It is not for me to judge. This is in the hands of our Lord. It is for me to say that salvation is by grace.

"For by grace are ye saved through faith; and that not of yourselves: it is the gift of God:

"Not of works, lest any man should boast."—Eph. 2:8,9.

We will doubtless be surprised at some who gave such evidence of being saved, who were not saved at all. Some who were prominent in the work of the churches will not be caught up at the coming of our Lord. We may miss some deacons and some Sunday school teachers and some choir singers and some ushers and instrumentalists.

Yes, and we will doubtless be surprised to see some who are there: ordinary, humble folks, but folks who had put their faith in Jesus Christ, the Son of God.

I talked to a big marine on Friday night after our Fellowship Banquet. He said, "I do not know whether I am saved or not." With the Bible before us, he settled the matter. He said, "I know that Christ is my Saviour. I know that all is well with my soul."

On yesterday I talked with a big man in the office. He too said that he was not sure about his salvation, but before he left the office, he had settled the matter and said, "I know that Christ is mine."

This is the important matter that you must consider now: do you know Jesus Christ? Is He your Saviour? It is not a matter of church membership or baptism. It is not a matter of good works or personal morality. It is a matter of your relationship unto God through Jesus Christ the Saviour.

"Neither is there salvation in any other: for there is none other name under heaven given among men, whereby we must be saved."—Acts 4:12.

"Concerning Them Which Are Asleep"

"But I would not have you to be ignorant, brethren, concerning them which are asleep, that ye sorrow not, even as others which have not hope."—I Thess. 4:13.

No corner is safe from the dripping rain of earth's tears. Death is the skeleton at every feast, the bitterness in every cup, the discord in our music, the nameless dread that has haunted man from the time sorrow had its first birthplace, in a mother's broken heart, as she knelt by the side of her boy, murdered through the passionate violence of his own brother (Lockyer).

The Bible plainly declares, "It is appointed unto men once to die, but after this the judgment" (Heb. 9:27). Death is a fact we have to face. Death is stalking our streets, our highways, our nation, and our world every moment of every day.

A bright word appears in the Scriptures; it is this: some will never die. One generation, alive at the coming of Christ, will not die. Here is the promise:

"Then we which are alive and remain shall be caught up together with them in the clouds, to meet the Lord in the air: and so shall we ever be with the Lord."—I Thess. 4:17.

Don't laugh at death! Death is certain—if He tarries. No really thoughtful man will speak lightly of death. Christ may come at any moment, but still we must face the fact of death as it is in this present hour.

The Bible gives a number of expressions relative to those who die with their faith in Christ.

"Abraham's bosom"—Luke 16:22. This speaks of the comfort the believer has in the Lord.

"In paradise"—Luke 23:43. Jesus said, "To day shalt thou be with me in paradise." This points to the fact of the presence of God immediately at death.

"Under the altar"—Revelation 6:9. This signifies the complete security of those "that were slain for the word of God, and for the testimony which they held."

"Sleep" is the usual designation for the death of believers and applies only to the body.

"He said unto them, Give place: for the maid is not dead, but sleepeth. And they laughed him to scorn."—Matt. 9:24.

"These things said he: and after that he saith unto them, Our friend Lazarus sleepeth; but I go, that I may awake him out of sleep."—John 11:11.

"And he kneeled down, and cried with a loud voice, Lord, lay not this sin to their charge. And when he had said this, he fell asleep."—Acts 7:60.

"For David, after he had served his own generation by the will of God, fell on sleep, and was laid unto his fathers, and saw corruption."—Acts 13:36.

Jesus referred to death as sleep. So did the Apostle Paul.

"For if we believe that Jesus died and rose again, even so them also which sleep in Jesus will God bring with him."—I Thess. 4:14.

What did Jesus mean by the word "sleep"? He said, "Lazarus sleepeth" and "the maid sleepeth." What was He saying to us?

He was not saying that the soul was asleep, nor that it was unconscious. The appearance of Moses and Elijah on the Mount of Transfiguration shows clearly that the souls of the departed are conscious.

In Luke 16 our Saviour points out soul-consciousness of both the lost and the saved. We are permitted to look into the abode of the blessed and the abode of the wicked.

Now, again we turn to the portion of Scripture we are using for this series.

". . .*concerning them which are asleep. . . .*
". . .*even so them also which sleep in Jesus will God bring
with him.*

"*For this we say unto you by the word of the Lord, that we
which are alive and remain unto the coming of the Lord shall not
prevent* [the better word is precede] *them which are asleep.*"—I
Thess. 4:13-15.

The Bible speaks much of sleeping—what does the Word of
God mean by this? I believe we can answer the question in three
ways.

Sleeping means life. When you go to sleep, you are still alive.
Your blood is circulating. When death comes, the body sleeps.
The soul is alive and conscious.

Sleeping means rest. When death comes and the body sleeps,
it is resting from the sorrows and heartaches of this life. The soul
is conscious and is with the Lord. The body is resting.

Sleeping means awaking. When we go to bed to sleep, we expect to awaken in the morning. When we die, the body sleeps.
The soul is in the presence of the Lord. When the Lord comes,
the sleeping body arises from the grave. The eternal soul in the
presence of Christ is joined with the resurrection body—"and so
shall we ever be with the Lord."

Now with this introduction in mind, let me suggest three very
simple thoughts.

I. GOD CARES FOR HIS OWN

He provides for His children. He provides all of our needs day
by day, and He provides for our eternal needs.

We need not fear death. Paul said in II Corinthians 5:8, "We
are confident, I say, and willing rather to be absent from the
body, and to be present with the Lord." William Evans, a Bible
teacher of years gone by, said that we might paraphrase this
verse in the words, "Therefore, we have a cheerful view of
death."

Yes, we can have a cheerful view of death when we remember
what our Lord has done for us. Christ died upon the cross that we

might have life everlasting. This life is obtained by simple faith in the Lord Jesus.

How beautifully did Jesus speak of death! Lazarus died and Jesus said, "Lazarus sleepeth."

Here is what the Saviour said to the Apostle John in the Revelation:

"Fear not; I am the first and the last:

"I am he that liveth, and was dead; and, behold, I am alive for evermore, Amen; and have the keys of hell and of death."—Rev. 1:17,18.

As we think of death, we must remember that our Lord cares for His own. The love of God must be brought into every consideration of this matter of death.

We must know that God in His great love for us has sent to us the message of the coming of our Saviour. What is this message? It is that Christ will come. The dead in Christ will arise, and the living will be changed.

Paul wrote to the church in Corinth,

"Behold, I shew you a mystery; We shall not all sleep, but we shall all be changed,

"In a moment, in the twinkling of an eye, at the last trump: for the trumpet shall sound, and the dead shall be raised incorruptible, and we shall be changed."—I Cor. 15:51,52.

The promise of the second coming is established; and when He comes, we shall be caught up into His presence—"and so shall we ever be with the Lord."

II. GOD LOVES THE SINNER

The death of Christ is the manifestation of God's love. Jesus said, "For God so loved the world, that he gave his only begotten Son, that whosoever believeth in him should not perish, but have everlasting life."

Paul wrote to the people of Rome, "But God commendeth his love toward us, in that, while we were yet sinners, Christ died for us" (Rom. 5:8). As we contemplate the matter of life and death and the future, we would remember certain things.

First, God knows the eternity of the soul of man. He made man, and He knows what is in man. Man is an eternal soul. That soul will live on throughout eternity. In the presence of God, the soul of man will enjoy blessedness and peace. In the place called Hell, "prepared for the devil and his angels," the soul will have only suffering forever and forever. God knows the soul of men. Hence, we should understand the great love that God has for the sinner.

Second, God knows the awfulness of Hell. The suffering of Hell is known to the Father. In this Book, the Bible, we are told of Hell and its suffering. In the account of Hell given by the Lord Jesus recorded in Luke 16, we find the story of the rich man. He died and went to Hell. In Hell he said, "I am tormented in this flame." I remind you that this is the Word of our Saviour.

Again, we find a picture of the awfulness of Hell in Matthew 25:41.

"Then shall he say also unto them on the left hand, Depart from me, ye cursed, into everlasting fire, prepared for the devil and his angels."

God has done His best to save men. He sent His Son to die for us. The Saviour shed His blood upon the cross, fulfilling God's requirement for salvation. "And almost all things are by the law purged with blood; and without shedding of blood is no remission" (Heb. 9:22).

God gave His Son that we might have life. God has given us the Bible to be a barricade to Hell. The Bible warns men of the awfulness of Hell, and the Bible plainly points the way to life everlasting. God has spread around this world gospel churches, many faithful preachers, and thousands of missionaries all with one task—to tell the story of salvation through Jesus Christ. God loves the sinner!

III. WE MUST FACE DEATH

I remind you again that Jesus may come at any moment; but if He tarries, then death will strike every person in this audience.

We will come to "walk through the valley of the shadow of death."

We need to face death as the Word teaches. Man in the vigor of life shouts out his bravadoes against death; but as he draws near to the end of the way, it is a different story.

There is one preparation and that is for man to turn to Christ, receive Him as Saviour, and know that in Him we have life, for He is "the resurrection and the life."

You cannot bribe death. All of your money and power cannot stay his work.

You cannot avoid death. Face it you must. You cannot tunnel around it nor fly over it.

You must face death, and you face death alone unless Jesus Christ is your Saviour.

The story is told of an aged woman who lay dying. By her bedside with his hand in hers sat the man who for over fifty years had been her husband. Her life was failing fast and eternity was drawing near to the aged woman. Grasping the hand of her husband tightly, she said, "John, it's getting dark. Take my hand. For over fifty years we have traveled together and you have led me. Now it is getting dark, and I cannot see the way. John, come with me, won't you?"

But John could not go; and with tear-filled eyes and trembling voice he said, "Anna, I cannot go. Only Jesus can go with you."

There is a story told of a little girl ten years of age. The angel of death was hovering over her bed. The end was drawing near. She said to her father, who was standing by the mother's side of the bed, "Daddy it is getting dark and I cannot see. Will you please go with me?"

With heart breaking, the father had to say, "Child, I cannot. I cannot go with you."

The girl turned to her mother and said, "Mamma, then you will, won't you?"

But the mother in turn, amidst her tears, replied, "Darling, I would, but I cannot. Only Jesus can go with you."

The Lord is enough. When you have Christ by your side, He takes away the fear of death.

The story has been told many times of D. L. Moody in his dying hours in his Northfield home. It is said that he awoke out of sleep about seven o'clock in the morning and was heard to say, "Earth recedes. Heaven opens before me. It is beautiful. It is like a trance. If this is death, it is sweet. There is no valley here. God is calling me, and I must go."

At first the family thought he was dreaming. But he said, "No, this is no dream." And then he added, "This is my coronation day. I have been looking forward to it for years." Later his face lit up as he exclaimed, "Dwight, Irene; I see the children's faces" (He referred to his grandchildren who had gone on before him.)

Sinking into unconsciousness, he seemed for a while to have passed into the unseen world. But under the effect of heart stimulants, he revived; and suddenly raising himself up on his elbow, he exclaimed, "What does this mean? What are you all doing here? This is a strange thing. I have been beyond the gates of death to the very portals of Heaven, and here I am back again."

In answer to his daughter's plea not to leave them, he replied, "I'll stay as long as I can, but if my time has come, I am ready to go."

He insisted on leaving his bed and sitting in a chair. He said, "I can meet death in my chair as well as in the bed." He walked across the room and sat in his easy chair for a while. But another sinking spell seized him and he was willing to return to his bed. In a few minutes he "fell asleep" quietly and peacefully to join the heavenly choirs on the following Christmas morning.

I know that many of us can never do it, but wouldn't it be wonderful if we could face death and talk about death like D. L. Moody did, if we could talk about it cheerfully and gladly and without fear, if we could so speak about it that we would be a blessing to others around us?

There is only One who can give you peace, and that one is the Lord Jesus Christ.

I was preaching in Festus, Missouri, last evening. At the invitation, a number of people came forward. Then I noticed a preacher friend about midway of the building who turned to a

man by his side and said just a few words to him. The man left
his place and came to the front. He dropped upon his knees and
in a few moments he stood to his feet saying that he had been
saved.

The man who was saved was a prominent contractor in St.
Louis. He had gone by the preacher's home in St. Louis to talk to
him about a matter of business. The preacher urged him to come
with him to the service. He told him that he could not because he
still had on his work clothes. The preacher took him in the house,
gave him a shirt, a coat, some trousers and even a pair of dress
shoes. The man came and stood in the midst of the people. The
Spirit of God spoke to him. He walked down the aisle and ac-
cepted Jesus Christ as his Saviour.

I saw a man who was bubbling over with joy that he had come
to the Lord Jesus Christ. That man was not prepared for life, for
eternity, for death, for the second coming of Jesus Christ, until
he met Jesus and received Him as his Saviour.

You have heard me tell about the little family, the mother and
father and a small son. The parents were devout Christians. The
mother became ill and died. The father, thinking that he might
save his son from seeing the form of his dead mother, sent the
boy away to stay with some friends. The lad was not permitted to
attend the funeral.

When the father went by to pick up his boy, he told him that
his mother had gone away for a while. For a number of days, he
kept this up, telling the boy that Mother would be back; she had
just gone away for a time.

Then one evening past the midnight hour the father could not
sleep. He was troubled by the lies that he had been telling his
boy. As he told the story, he said, "I heard footsteps. I knew that
that was my boy. He had gotten out of his bed and was coming
into my room. In a few moments his hands touched my bed and
he said, 'Daddy, may I get in with you?' I told him yes. He lay
there quietly for a moment. Then he said, 'Daddy, I'd like to ask
you once more. When will Mamma be home?' "

He said, "For some reason I became angry and shouted in the
darkness of the night, 'Your mother will not come home! She is

dead. You will not see her again in this world. We will not see her until we get to Heaven.' "

He said, "My boy began to sob. I thought his heart would break. After a while the sobs died away. And in a few moments I heard him say, 'Daddy, I want to ask you one more question.' I could not refuse him. I said, 'Yes, Son, what is it?'

" 'Daddy, is your face toward me?' " He said, "I replied, 'Yes, Son, my face is toward you.' "

He said, "In a little while the boy was asleep. Then I left the bed and stood by the window. I looked out into the night and saw the stars in the heavens. I could only say one thing: 'Dear Father, there is just one thing that I want to ask. 'Is Your face toward me? If Your face is toward me, then I can stand the sorrow, and I can go on.' "

My friend, is God your Father? Is Heaven your home? Do you feel His presence with you?

The Greatest Prospect in the World

"*. . .and so shall we ever be with the Lord.*"—I Thess. 4:17b.

What glorious finality is sounded in the words of Paul! He has presented the coming of Christ in detail. He has spoken of the resurrection of believers and the translation of the living. Why? ". . .to meet the Lord in the air." And then he adds: ". . .and so shall we ever be with the Lord."

Paul was presenting to the Christians in Thessalonica the greatest prospect that he could imagine—to be with the Lord.

It is amazing how the prospect of certain things can inspire the soul. When we are anticipating events and attainments, we press on! We are not deterred by the consideration of illness. We are not disturbed too much by opposition. We have before us a glorious prospect and we want to reach it.

Some men are driven forward by the prospect of riches. Too often when success is secured, it brings meager joy.

Some men are attracted by position. It may be political. It may be educational. It may be social. A high position, though attained, may bring but little satisfaction.

Some people are attracted by power. They want the place of power. They sacrifice much. They discount health, friends and pleasures to attain power. They strive for the place of leadership.

Others are driven forward by the desire for popularity. This is the motivating force in back of their lives.

But, oh, the failure of *things*! How plainly did Jesus speak unto us: "But seek ye first the kingdom of God, and his righteousness; and all these things shall be added unto you" (Matt. 6:33).

Men may gain money, but it often brings its heartaches.

Men may gain popularity and discover that it is nothing but ashes.

Men may build what they feel is a good life—spend much time in hard work—striving, and then find that it is nothing. Too often the attainments bring little joy because of that which happens in the hour of fruition.

For example, a man of our city spent a full lifetime working at his job. He accomplished something in a financial way. He came to the age of retirement, and he decided to spend the remaining years of his life in Florida. He told his family that he thought he would have a physical checkup before leaving the city. The examination revealed that he had cancer. He lived but a short time after his retirement.

Now the Apostle Paul is suggesting to us a glorious finality for the Christian life. He places before the believer the highest joy that he could imagine. What was it? It is found in the text of our message: ". . .and so shall we ever be with the Lord."

The second coming of Christ is before us. In the light of our text, what does His coming mean?

I. HIS COMING MEANS HIS PRESENCE

". . .and so shall we ever be with the Lord."

What a great prospect is this—we are going to see Him!

In His presence! With Him forever! Ah, this brings to light a thought that we had better consider. If you do not like the Lord's presence now, it is a sure thing that you will not like it later. If you are not consumed with a great joy and happiness in the fellowship of God's people, in the reading of the Word, in prayer, in soul winning, in the work of our Lord, it is doubtful that you will like His presence. (But perhaps we need not worry about this. If a person does not like the presence of the Lord now, if he does not care for the work of God in this hour, then it may be doubtful that that individual has ever been saved.)

Simon Peter was weak and sinful, but he loved the presence of Christ. When he denied his Lord and the cock crew, the Bible says, "And Peter went out, and wept bitterly." He loved the presence of Christ. He was among the first to come to the sepulchre. He listened to the words of our Lord Jesus; and though his life had been marked with stumbling and failures, he was a preacher on the day of Pentecost.

There are three suggestions that I would give to help us in this matter:

First, daily sense His presence. The Apostle Paul did, and he wrote to the churches in Galatia, "Christ liveth in me." John sensed the presence of Jesus and wrote to the "little children" saying, "If we love one another, God dwelleth in us, and his love is perfected in us" (I John 4:12).

It would help every child of God listening to me this morning to spend some time every day quietly waiting upon the presence of the Lord. This is what David had in mind when he said, "Rest in the Lord, and wait patiently for him."

Too many Christians have never taken the time to wait quietly upon God and to feel His divine presence.

Perhaps the pastor was not far wrong in the thing that he did quite often. He said that he would go to his study and place a chair in the center of the room and seat himself in another chair before the empty one. And then he said that he would endeavor to sense the presence of God. He said he tried to feel that the Lord was speaking to him and giving him guidance for the work of that day.

Second, we must know that we shall see Him one day face to face. John said, ". . .but we know that, when he shall appear, we shall be like him; for we shall see him as he is." Christ is coming. This is established in the holy, infallible, inerrant Word of God. He is coming to receive us unto Himself. He is coming to bring us into His presence. He said, "I will come again, and receive you unto myself; that where I am, there ye may be also." We must receive this plain Word of God and know that one day we shall see Him face to face.

It would do us good to contemplate that which is coming. I have observed that strong Christians are made by contemplation of the coming of Christ. It is time well spent to think over what it means when we shall stand before our blessed Lord.

As we think of seeing Him face to face, I am reminded of the old story of the young girl who broke away from a country home and drifted into the city. The distracted mother sought everywhere to find her daughter. In her search she came to a rescue mission and told the story to the superintendent of the mission. She said, "Can you find my daughter for me?"

He replied, "If she is in the city, I think I can, if you will do what I tell you."

She said, "I will do anything to get my daughter back again."

The superintendent said, "Go to the photographer and have him take your picture. Bring me one hundred large-sized pictures of yourself."

The mother did as she was directed. She brought them back to the superintendent. He said, "Now sit down and write underneath every picture just two words, 'Come home.' Then you may go home and wait God's time, praying that He may help us find your daughter."

The godly man put the pictures in one hundred places of sin. A few nights later a group of merrymakers came into one of the places. In the group was that daughter. Her eyes were attracted to the picture on the wall. There was something about it that looked familiar.

Stepping across the room, she recognized it as a picture of her mother. She saw the picture. She saw the writing of the two words at the bottom of the picture—"Come home." The invitation written in the familiar hand of her mother and the sweet face of a Christian mother touched the heart of the girl. She fled from her escorts and took the first train back to her home. In a few hours she had made her confession, sought and found conviction. She came back to God, back to the Saviour, and back to her mother's arms.

I use that illustration just to drive home the fact that one day we shall see Him face to face.

Third, we must know that we shall be with Him throughout eternity. I repeat the text, ". . .and so shall we ever be with the Lord." He is coming. We shall meet Him in the air. We shall stand before the judgment seat of Christ. We shall take part in the marriage supper of the Lamb. We shall come with Him in His revelation and reign with Him for a thousand years upon this earth. Then will come the new heavens and the new earth, life forevermore in the presence of our Saviour.

II. HIS COMING MEANS HIS PLACE

He is coming again, and we shall reign with Him. "Do ye not know that the saints shall judge the world? and if the world shall be judged by you, are ye unworthy to judge the smallest matters?" (I Cor. 6:2).

He comes to receive us unto Himself, and He comes to reign upon the earth; and we come to reign with Him.

"And hast made us unto our God kings and priests: and we shall reign on the earth."—Rev. 5:10.

". . .and they lived and reigned with Christ a thousand years."—Rev. 20:4.

Christ is coming to be the King of kings and the Lord of lords. In the millennial reign, He will be the sole object of worship. He will combine in harmony His kingly and priestly functions.

He is coming as the Son of God, the Son of man and the Son of David; as He reigns upon the earth, He will combine all that He was and all that He is. He will reign without a rival. This entire planet will be His domain, and His throne will be in Jerusalem.

He will reign and all people will know Him. Listen to this word in Philippians 2:9-11:

"Wherefore God also hath highly exalted him, and given him a name which is above every name:

"That at the name of Jesus every knee should bow, of things in heaven, and things in earth, and things under the earth;

"And that every tongue should confess that Jesus Christ is Lord, to the glory of God the Father."

In the day of His millennial reign, none will be able to say that they do not know Him. From the least to the greatest, He will be revealed in all His glory.

"They shall not hurt nor destroy in all my holy mountain: for

the earth shall be full of the knowledge of the Lord, as the waters cover the sea."—Isa. 11:9.

His coming means His place; our place will be at His side. Let me suggest a few things that this will mean.

First, fear will be gone. Fear of death. Fear of others. Fear of unpleasantness. Fear of need. How often Jesus said to the disciples, "Fear not." How often He speaks to us and gives that word of encouragement, "Fear not." Yet in spite of all that our Saviour says to us, in spite of every promise in the Bible, we still have fears.

A very fine student of Tennessee Temple came in to see me sometime ago. He stated very frankly that he had a few troubles, that he was worried about things. He said, "I have my bill paid for all of this year, but, I am troubled now about the bill for next year." I told him that he should live one day at a time and have faith in God. I tried to describe the result of our faith in Him. Faith takes away fear. I am not sure that I succeeded, but I trust he was helped.

Fear is a common thing in this day, but fear will be gone in His presence and in His place.

Second, uncertainty will be gone. When we reign with Him upon the earth, we will know what is right and what is wrong.

The present world is one of uncertainty. Our nation is fighting a thousand battles. But the biggest battle is the battle with fear and uncertainty. We fought a war overseas, in Viet Nam. Eighteen thousand young men gave their lives in that war. The tragedy of it all was the uncertainty. People are not quite sure what we were doing, what we were fighting for, and what victories we had hoped to win.

Somehow it needed to be stated the purpose for which we were fighting. Such a statement would have taken away much uncertainty. I am quite aware of the threat of communism and the usual answers that are given to the matter of war. But there needed to be a more comprehensive answer for the hearts of people.

Now we find an uncertainty in Palestine. Matters are not fully settled between Israel and the Arabs.

Uncertainty is a descriptive word for this day and age. It goes all the way from the garbage collectors in New York City to the congressmen in the House and Senate and to the striking educators in Florida.

Third, when we come into His presence, weakness will be gone. We shall have His strength. There is a strength that is given us now, mentioned in Isaiah 40:31:

"But they that wait upon the Lord shall renew their strength; they shall mount up with wings as eagles; they shall run, and not be weary; and they shall walk, and not faint."

There is a strength by waiting upon God. This is promised to all of us. But when we come into His presence, we shall have the strength that will abide forever.

Fourth, our place at His side will mean that death will be gone. As I dictate this message, a beautiful little girl three years of age is hovering between life and death. The distraught parents are standing by, praying and hoping. Many friends are praying with them, but it seems that death is standing just outside the door.

In another hospital of our city, a man lingers between life and death.

Death is an everyday happening. One day it shall be no more.

Today the rich and the poor die. The young and the old die. Death is common. Some years ago Senator Clark received a telegram from his son announcing the birth of a child. The senator so rejoiced over being the grandfather of a baby boy that he sent a million-dollar check as a gift to the new heir.

A few days later when the baby's mother was suffering from blood poisoning, specialists were rushed from Chicago, St. Paul and Denver to the Clark home in Montana. They did all they could to save her life. The physicians had a consultation about her case. They did their best. Then they turned to the anxious husband and said, "There is no hope, Mr. Clark. Your wife will die."

It is reported that he drew from his pocket the million-dollar check which had been given him by his father for the baby. He threw it on the table by the doctor, saying, "A mother is worth more to a boy than millions. Save my wife and the money is yours."

They said, "We cannot do it."

To this the husband replied, "Save her, men, and you shall have the money and a copper mine." But they could not do it. The wife of the millionaire miner soon passed away.

At His side, death will be no more!

But keep in mind the millennial kingdom is just the beginning of all that we have in Christ. Not only will we reign with Him for a thousand years, but we are coming into the new heavens and the new earth "wherein dwelleth righteousness."

"For, behold, I create new heavens and a new earth: and the former shall not be remembered, nor come into mind."—Isa. 65:17.

"For as the new heavens and the new earth, which I will make, shall remain before me, saith the Lord, so shall your seed and your name remain."—Isa. 66:22.

"Nevertheless we, according to his promise, look for new heavens and a new earth, wherein dwelleth righteousness."—II Pet. 3:13.

"And I saw a new heaven and a new earth: for the first heaven and the first earth were passed away; and there was no more sea."—Rev. 21:1.

His coming means His place. We shall be with our Saviour. Fear, uncertainty, weakness and death will be no more. We shall reign with Him.

III. HIS COMING MEANS HIS PEACE

In this restless and troubled age, there is a universal longing for peace. Multitudes of fevered, troubled lives are seeking the repose that only a gracious God can give. We are often asking, "Is there peace for this war-weary, blood-soaked earth?" We need to see this truth: There is a peace, and that peace is in Him.

In this present day there will continue to be "wars and rumours of wars." In spite of all the dreamings of man, war continues. The president of our nation and leaders of other nations join together in talking about everlasting peace coming to the earth. They think that peace will come by war, but not so. Peace will come with the Lord Jesus Christ.

Wars will continue because of the sinful nature of man. War will continue until the coming of Jesus because the Devil is loose and the Devil is a deceiver and a malicious troublemaker, an enemy of God.

But, my friend, His coming means His peace. Peace will come to this earth. Peace will come to the nations. Peace will come to the families.

But I hasten to say that there is peace for you now if you will but receive it.

First, there is peace through salvation. Sin can bring only heartaches, but when man surrenders to the Lord Jesus and by repentance and faith puts his trust in Christ, then he receives salvation and will also receive peace for his heart. The cross reconciles the sinner to God. Christ died in the sinner's place. He made the atonement for us so that we might be at peace with God.

Now, let us remember that this blood-bought peace is not an intangible something. This peace is a *Person,* even Jesus Christ the Son of God. Romans 5:1 reads, "Therefore being justified by faith, we have peace with God through our Lord Jesus Christ." Someone said, "A sin-hating God met the sin-bearing Christ at Calvary and there and then made a full settlement of the sin question."

Second, there is peace through the will of God. No one will enjoy the fullness of peace until there is surrender. We must accept God's will for our lives, and then "the peace of God, which passeth all understanding, shall keep your hearts and minds through Christ Jesus."

Third, there is peace in the work of God. Many hundreds of you would testify to the fact that you have found peace through obedience to Christ and the doing of His work. The reason for the restless souls of many professing Christians is very simple. They are not doing anything for Christ. Peace will come when we speak for the Saviour, worship the Saviour, live for the Saviour,

and lay ourselves out for the extension of His work around the
world.

Fourth, there is peace in anticipation of the future. We are facing the imminent return of Jesus Christ. He may come at any
moment and glorious events will begin to take place; through our
faith in Him, we will participate in all that is promised to us in
the Word of God. Christ is coming! Are you ready for His coming?

Finally, there is peace through total faith and trust in Him.
". . .faith cometh by hearing, and hearing by the word of God."
We must have faith in Jesus for salvation, and we must have
faith in Him for a victorious walk with Him day by day.

I was thrilled by the reading of a paragraph from a book written some years ago.

> When the messenger of death said to Patrick Henry, the hero
> of colonial times, that death was near, Henry said to his physi-
> cian, "Doctor, sit by and I will show you how a Christian can
> die."

When death came to the mother of Talmage, her eleven
children were safe in the fold of Jesus. She prayed, "Now, Lord,
lettest Thou Thy servant depart in peace; for mine eyes have
seen Thy salvation." That petition was soon answered.

Daniel Webster, the great leader of our republic of bygone
days, said to those in his room in the hour of death:

> My general wish on earth has been to do my Master's will.
> That there is a God all must acknowledge. What would be the
> condition of any of us if we had not the hope of immortality?
> Thank God! The Gospel of Jesus Christ brought immortality to
> light.

Then with a prayer upon his lips, he passed away as peacefully
as a child going to sleep.

The aunt of Gipsy Smith lay dying in an old gypsy camp and
she said, "Tell the world I have found Jesus to be a rock in a
weary land, a shelter in the time of storm." She passed from that
gypsy tent to Heaven.

President McKinley came to the time of death. He said to his
physicians, "It is useless, Gentlemen. I think we ought to have

prayer." With a smile on his countenance, the president led in prayer while the surgeons and the nurses were in tears. With a prayer upon his lips, he departed to be with God.

Thank God for the truth of the coming of Jesus Christ! His coming means peace. Peace can be yours today: peace through salvation; peace through the will of God; peace in the work of God; peace in anticipation of the future; and peace through total faith and trust in Him.

I bid you to come to the Lord and receive Him as your Saviour, and know for your heart the peace of God.

"Comfort Ye My People"
or
The Sweetest Comfort in
the World

"Wherefore comfort one another with these words."—I Thess. 4:18.

Paul was a mighty preacher of the second coming of Jesus Christ. To the disturbed Thessalonians he repeated this theme— Christ is coming!

"And to wait for his Son from heaven, whom he raised from the dead, even Jesus, which delivered us from the wrath to come."— I Thess. 1:10.

"For what is our hope, or joy, or crown of rejoicing? Are not even ye in the presence of our Lord Jesus Christ at his coming?

"For ye are our glory and joy."—I Thess. 2:19,20.

* * *

"To the end he may stablish your hearts unblameable in holiness before God, even our Father, at the coming of our Lord Jesus Christ with all his saints."—I Thess. 3:13.

* * *

"For the Lord himself shall descend from heaven with a shout, with the voice of the archangel, and with the trump of God: and the dead in Christ shall rise first:

"Then we which are alive and remain shall be caught up together with them in the clouds, to meet the Lord in the air: and so shall we ever be with the Lord."—I Thess. 4:16,17.

"And the very God of peace sanctify you wholly; and I pray

God your whole spirit and soul and body be preserved blameless
unto the coming of our Lord Jesus Christ."—I Thess. 5:23.

The believers in Thessalonica had been asking questions:
"What is taking place? What about our loved ones who are dying? What is God doing? What should we do? When will Christ
come?"

Paul gave the answers. He told them that Christ is coming,
and when He comes the dead in Christ will be raised, the living
changed, and together we shall be caught up in the clouds to
meet the Lord, "and so shall we ever be with the Lord." Now
after these declarations, Paul wrote to them, "Wherefore comfort
one another with these words."

Here is comfort for everyone! The amazing Lord gives comfort
to every soul. Each person needs a peculiar type of comfort. You
need comfort of a certain kind, and I need another kind. God
gives us what we need. Psalm 23 ministers to many hearts, John
14 ministers to others, I Corinthians 15 to others, I Thessalonians
4 to some people, Revelation 21 to others.

But it seems that the apostle felt that here were some amazing
words that would give comfort to all people. Therefore he said,
by inspiration of the Holy Spirit, "Wherefore comfort one
another with these words."

We do not find comfort in money nor in position nor in popularity. There is little comfort in the subjects of death and judgment, and of course, there is no comfort in the subject of Hell.
But there is comfort in the fact of His coming again!

There are three things that I want you to see in this message of
comfort.

I. THIS TROUBLED WORLD

The Christian is not promised an easy time in this present
world.

Jesus said:

"Blessed are ye when men shall revile you, and persecute you,
and shall say all manner of evil against you falsely, for my sake.

"Rejoice, and be exceeding glad: for great in your reward in

heaven: for so persecuted they the prophets which were before you."—Matt. 5:11,12.

This is a troubled world, and sin is the trouble! Every trouble, every heartache, every pain, every grave—all evil stems from sin.

War and bloodshed come from sin. Broken homes are the result of sin. Distressed minds are the consequences of Satan and sin.

But there are some troubles you need never fear.

You need not fear regarding your needs. Why? God has promised to provide for every need that you might have. The Apostle Paul said, "But my God shall supply all your need according to his riches in glory by Christ Jesus" (Phil. 4:19).

Jesus said to the disciples that "your heavenly Father knoweth that ye have need of all these things" (Matt. 6:32).

The promises of God cover every need and trial of life. It is for us to search them out, to claim them as our own, and to rest upon them in the time of trouble.

A woman who was lost in the rocky desert of the Rio Grande Valley for six days remained amazingly calm and confident throughout the ordeal. She located a little cave with a trickling stream of water and waited quietly until she was found. "I kept repeating the 23rd Psalm," she explained after her rescue, "and I always felt that someone would find me."

Isaiah tells us, "Thou wilt keep him in perfect peace, whose mind is stayed on thee: because he trusteth in thee" (Isa. 26:3). The psalmist tells us, "This poor man cried, and the Lord heard him, and saved him out of all his troubles" (Ps. 34:6).

Second, you need not fear regarding God's guidance. He has promised to guide you every step of the way. His guidance will be given to the submissive and willing Christian. One of our strongest examples in this field is in the experience of the Apostle Paul. The Lord gave him guidance for every day. He closed one door and opened another. Simply lay yourself out before God and with a submissive heart ask for His guidance.

Third, you need not fear about God's presence. He has promised, "I will never leave thee nor forsake thee." I think some days that our fears are pretty large. They are like the boy who came to our home to deliver the evening paper. Our dog King happened to be loose, and he took after the boy. The boy became exceedingly frightened; and I know he manifested his fear. This gave the dog extra courage, and he grabbed hold of the boy and pushed him up in a corner of the porch. That boy had a "king-sized fear."

There are some fears that are justifiable and good for us. There are many fears, however, that we should not have. Jesus often admonished His disciples, "Fear not."

The psalmist said, "I sought the Lord, and he heard me, and delivered me from all my fears." We can be delivered from fear when we live in the companionship of Jesus Christ. We must practice His presence in our daily living. We can bring Him into every situation of our lives.

Again, we can turn our fears over to Him. This means confessing of the fears one by one and asking Him to remove them and give us grace in the hours of trial.

And, of course, we can apply the Word of God to every fear that arises. If there is a time of danger, we can claim Psalm 91:11, "For he shall give his angels charge over thee, to keep thee in all thy ways." If we are facing failure, we need to lay hold on Philippians 4:13, "I can do all things through Christ which strengtheneth me."

In the time of severe troubles, we can say, "God is our refuge and strength, a very present help in trouble."

If we are disturbed about the matter of death, we can lay hold upon Psalm 23:4, "Yea, though I walk through the valley of the shadow of death, I will fear no evil: for thou art with me; thy rod and thy staff they comfort me."

In a gospel tract I saw these words:

> Many years ago there was a little boy on a trundle bed who had just retired for the night. Before going to sleep, he turned in the direction of the large bed on which his father lay and said, "Father, are you there?" And the answer came back, "Yes, my son." That boy turned over and went to sleep without a thought of harm.
>
> At this time that boy is a man of seventy, and every night before going to sleep he looks up into the face of his Heavenly

Father and says, "Father, are you there?" And the answer comes back, "Yes, my son." And then he asks in childish faith, "Will You take care of me tonight?" And the answer comes back clear and strong, "Yes, my son. I will never leave thee nor forsake thee."

My friend, you need not fear about God's presence. He will be with you.

Fourth, you need not fear regarding His return. The promise of our Saviour has been given: "I will come again." He tells us to watch and be ready for His coming. Many times our Saviour spoke of His return. Then we find His promises echoed by the Apostle Paul, even as we read them here in First Thessalonians.

The time of His return is in the Father's hands, but the promise has been given by the one who cannot lie.

II. THIS TEMPORARY WORLD

We sing in the song, "Change and decay in all around I see. Oh, Thou who changest not, abide with me."

Jesus said, "Heaven and earth shall pass away, but my words shall not pass away" (Matt. 24:35).

The world likes to say that everything continues as it ever has. The scoffers say, "Where is the promise of his coming? For since the fathers fell sleep, all things continue as they were from the beginning of the creation." Men speak scoffingly, "You talk of the second coming. He has not come, and He will not come."

The lost world knows not the Word, nor has the lost world ever considered all that God has done in the past.

I like to read Hebrews 13:8, "Jesus Christ the same yesterday, and to day, and for ever."

Christ is ever the same, but we are facing some momentous events in the future.

First, Christ is coming. He is coming to receive us unto Himself. This is the part of the second coming that we call the rapture. The dead in Christ shall rise first. The living will be changed, and together we shall be caught up in the air to meet our Lord.

The rapture of the saints will bring to pass that which Jesus said, "Then shall two be in the field; the one shall be taken, and the other left" (Matt. 24:40). What changes will be made in this world at the coming of our Saviour!

Second, not only is Christ coming, but the Great Tribulation is coming to this earth. When the saints of God are caught up into the air and when the Holy Spirit is caught up with the saints, there will come a Great Tribulation.

"For then shall be great tribulation, such as was not since the beginning of the world to this time, no, nor ever shall be."— Matt. 24:21.

This is the time of great untold suffering upon a Christ-rejecting world. A full description of the Great Tribulation comes to us in the book of Revelation, chapter 4, and extends into chapter 19. The graphic pictures given touch both the happenings as the saints of God are standing before the judgment seat of Christ and are partaking of the marriage supper of the Lamb, and the unparalleled suffering taking place upon the earth at the same time. The seven seals will be opened. The seven trumpets will be sounded. The seven vials will be poured out upon the earth.

The world does not remain the same. This is a changing world, and the greatest changes are yet in the future.

Third, the golden age is coming. This will be the millennial reign of Jesus upon the earth. Christ will come from the skies with His followers. He will fight the battle of Armageddon, direct the happenings of the judgment of living nations, and establish His reign upon the earth.

Now in the midst of all the changing situations, there is One who remains the same, and that One is Christ. Men must face the Lord Jesus. The children of God will come before Him at the judgment seat of Christ. Nations will stand before Him at the judgment of living nations. The lost will stand before Him at the Great White Throne Judgment.

A few hours ago they had a great meeting of the Black Muslims in Chicago. The newspaper told of how one man extolled Elijah

Muhammad. (This one is the head of the Black Muslims. He said the following:

> Elijah is greater than Booker T. Washington. I am not taking anything away from Booker T. Washington when I say this. Elijah Muhammad is greater than Abraham, greater than Moses, greater than Jesus.

As he made this statement, the eleven thousand people present shouted their approval. Among the eleven thousand were two thousand berobed women of the Muhammad's Sisterhood of Allah.

How gracious and longsuffering is our God, that He will allow poor sinners to exalt the name of mortal man above the name of the eternal Son of God! God in His patience allows it to go on now, but one day Christ will be the King of kings and Lord of lords. Every prophecy given of our Saviour will be fulfilled.

III. THIS FORTUNATE WORLD

This is a world of sin; it is a world headed for destruction; but this is still a fortunate world. Why? Because the message of the good news is still being proclaimed in this world. How thrilling it is that we can still teach the Gospel, preach the Gospel and sing the Gospel! I repeat, how fortunate is this world!

We, too, are fortunate. We have the glorious opportunity to proclaim the message of Christ. We must give the message at home. We must give it abroad. The entire world will never be saved, but this is the age when the Gospel is being preached and the called-out ones are responding. They are receiving Christ and walking in His steps.

My friend, the Gospel has never failed and it can never fail. God is accomplishing His purpose in this world. He is doing it with those who are repenting of their sins and believing in Jesus Christ for salvation.

I need to emphasize that it costs to carry the message of Christ. Jesus said,

"Verily, verily, I say unto you, Except a corn of wheat fall into the ground and die, it abideth alone: but if it die, it bringeth forth much fruit."—John 12:24.

Second, the glorious opportunity for service is ours. It is high time that we recognize the true meaning of service. Some people feel they are serving God only if they sing in the choir or teach a Sunday school class or work as an usher. This is not so. Your service for Christ may be a clean life, for by living such a life you are showing forth the power of the Son of God. By the radiance of your life, you are manifesting Christ to a lost world.

Again, your service may be a sincere word for Him, the testimony of your lips.

Your service may be a fearless attitude for Him. We may walk in the midst of an unregenerated world without apology and without compromise.

Yes, this is a fortunate world, for in this world there are men and women who are working for Christ and serving Him.

We are a fortunate world, for to this world will come our Saviour. Jesus said, "I will come again." This stirring thought must never leave us, but as the Father delays the coming of His Son, we have a job to do. We must proclaim the message of our Saviour.

The entire Bible proclaims the fact of the coming of Jesus.

Our Saviour repeated many times the promise of His return. In these mighty six verses we have before us in I Thessalonians 4, Paul is emphasizing to discouraged people the fact of the return of Jesus.

The sweetest comfort in this world is the thought of His coming. Someone put it in these words:

Last words are precious words. They carry the most weight. So it must have been with Jesus as He spoke this last promise by the Holy Spirit through John. He knew it was His final message, and what was the message? "Surely I come quickly. Amen."

Only five words, the number of grace, but they tell us five things.

SURELY speaks of the certainty of His coming.

I speaks of the personality of His coming.

COME tells us that it is not death we are to look for, but His personal return.

QUICKLY speaks of the time of His return. And since a

thousand years are as one day with the Lord, it is less than two days (in God's reckoning of time) since He left this promise. He will come quickly.

Then the promise ends with AMEN—the response of every child of God to His last promise. If Jesus should come today, would He find you ready with an "Amen. Even so, come, Lord Jesus"?

Now let us go back to the words of our text: "Wherefore comfort one another with these words." Paul is saying to the church in Thessalonica, "You will find comfort, ease of mind, and peace of heart in thinking upon the promise of His coming."

Now, what should we do? We should believe in the second coming. We are to talk about His coming; and we are to look for His coming.

There is one initial step that many of you need to take in order to be ready for His coming, and that is to receive Jesus Christ as your own personal Saviour. If you do not know Him as Saviour, you will be left when He comes. What a tragedy! The saved will be caught up; the unsaved will be left. You need Jesus, and you need Him right now.

Second, you need to be ready to stand before Him. The Bible says: "So then every one of us shall give account of himself to God" (Rom. 14:12). When we stand before the judgment seat, we want to be found faithful in the work that He has called us to do. God help us to be faithful!

A MANUAL
on Home and Family Living

The Home: Courtship, Marriage and Children

Dr. Rice covers almost every phase of the subject suggested by the title. In direct, spiritual language he gives what God says about the most intimate experiences of life that begin when young people come to the age of interest in the opposite sex, through courtship, marriage, the bringing of children into the world, and bringing up a family. Facts of nature, whispered and talked under the wrong environment, Dr. Rice meets face to face with wise and scriptural answers, without sidestepping the facts or dodging the issues.

Think of making an unchristian home Christian, a sad home happy, a perplexed and confused home happy and serene—a wrong home right! This book, by God's help, will do it!

THE HOME has become a handbook for homes, a manual for happy Christian living.

22 chapters, 381 large pages, hard binding, $5.50; paper binding, $1.95.

The MAN and His MINISTRY in Stories and Sermons

See his
birthplace;
church where
he was saved;
first pastor-
ate, etc.!

Colorful,
attractive
perfect
binding!

A new book by Dr. Lee Roberson. The book's title is a take-off from the author's characteristic, personalized double-breasted blue serge suit coat, choosing to make this symbolic of his lifelong twofold ministry as a pastor and an educator. The "double" theme of the title also suggests the twofold contents of the book: one section being autobiographical; the other section, sermonic. Lovers and acquaintances (and who in the ranks of present-day fundamentalism does not know this spiritual giant for God?) will be delighted with this charming volume. There are 20 brief autobiographical sketches; 10 blessed sermons. Treasurable pictorial middle section. 200 pages.

Two Other Success Books

Me? Obey Him?
By Elizabeth Rice Handford

Here is a book about women, for women, by a woman! It is tremendous! We doubt not that this book, placed in the right hands, could revolutionize a homelife that had been a hovel of misery and transform it into a haven of happiness. It could turn a defeated, frustrated, miserable wife into a happy, contented, excited helpmate. It could save many a home already on the verge of divorce. An investment in this book will pay big dividends. An ideal gift suggestion.

The Right Romance in Marriage
By Cathy Rice

This book has proven to be an extremely valuable one. Literally hundreds of letters have told of ruined marriages being saved from divorce courts, of dull marriages that have regained the fervor and excitement of honeymoon days and unhappy marriages that have found the answer to their problems. Many pastors now make it a practice to give a copy of this book to each couple they marry in order that the newlyweds may begin their life together.

TWO OF OUR LATEST BOOKS

Golden Moments With Dr. John R. Rice

A collection of devotional sermonettes taken from exact recordings as given by Dr. Rice to his staff of nearly 100 workers here at the Sword of the Lord. These devotionals are classified under various subject headings, and will prove helpful as devotional readings for the home circle. They give also an interesting insight into the tender, loving concern of a truly great man of God for his dedicated helpers in his great work of getting out the Gospel. 60 brief chapters; 304 pages. Paperback.

With Love. . .and a Pinch of Salt (for ladies)

By Jessie Rice Sandberg. This most recent volume by a gifted writer contains prescriptions for proper procedures in preparing for marriage; suggestions for both husbands and wives whereby they might strengthen the marriage bond; ideas for correction, discipline and training of children; etc.; together with a seemingly exhaustless collection of delicious, appetizing recipes, conveniently classified for ready use. 176 pages. Cloth.

You may use this as your order form, or order on separate paper.

Name _____

Address _____

City _____ State _____ Zip _____

John R. Rice Writes Right!

10 Messages That Changed 10,000 Lives

This man has been used of God to change the unsaved into saints, backsliders into useful tools, average preachers into great men of God. His ministry has changed people who are unaware of his influence. After you read these messages, you will have to say, "No wonder 10,000 lives were changed!" No doubt this figure is only a fraction of the number of people who have been influenced by these sermons. With rich illustrations, and with spiritual power. 264 pages.

Revival Appeals

16 of Dr. Rice's most powerfully used sermons to the unsaved. Like attending revival meetings! 216 pages.

What It Costs to Be a Good Christian

Multitudes would honestly like to live a fruitful, successful Christian life of service, but don't know how. Here is the Bible answer. 223 pages, cloth.

The Ruin of a Christian

This should be required reading for every Christian annually. 12 sermons to Christians. 253 pages.

You Must Be Born Again

Messages appealing to the unconverted: how to get salvation, how to keep it, and how to know it. Salvation sermons include: *Crossing the Deadline, Almost Persuaded, Today,* and *""At the Last."* 187 pages, 8 chapters.

Scarlet Sin and Other Revival Sermons, The

"Stirring revival sermons," reports the Baptist Standard, "with striking titles, soul-gripping illustrations, plain-spoken warning against sin . . . .They were preached for a verdict." 254 pages.

The Gospel That Has Saved 16,000 Souls

Yes, as the title suggests, "over 16,000 people have written that they found Christ through printed sermons by this author . . .," sermons such as are reproduced here in this big volume of 291 pages.

Earnestly Contending for the Faith

Here is the plainest Bible preaching you ever read, but with a tender heart, with holy faithfulness—the kind that has changed thousands of lives and won tens of thousands of souls. 16 chapters, 368 pages.